GW00367573

Other giftbooks by Helen Exley:

When Love is Forever   Words on Joy
The Kiss   Words on Kindness
Seize the Day!   Words on Love and Caring

Published simultaneously in 1998 by Exley Publications i
Great Britain, and Exley Publications LLC in the USA.
Copyright © Helen Exley 1998
MARION C. GARRETTY: published with permission
© Helen Exley 1998.
The moral right of the author has been asserted.

12 11 10 9 8 7 6

ISBN 1-86187-049-3

Quotations selected by Helen Exley.
Illustrated by Angela Kerr.
Printed in China.

**Exley Publications Ltd, 16 Chalk Hill, Watford,
Herts WD19 4BG, UK.
Exley Publications LLC, 185 Main Street, Spencer,
MA 01562, USA.
www.helenexleygiftbooks.com**

Love
MAKES
THE WORLD
GO ROUND

A HELEN EXLEY
GIFTBOOK

⧉EXLEY

*One word
frees us of
all the weight
and pain of
life: That
word is love.*

SOPHOCLES

Love lives
the moment;
it's neither
lost in
yesterday nor
does it crave
for tomorrow.
Love is Now!

LEO BUSCAGLIA

In

dreams

and in

love

there

are no

impossibilities.

JANUS ARONY

Love....
'Tis second life,
it grows into the
soul
Warms every
vein, and beats in
every pulse.

JOSEPH ADDISON

*A loving heart
carries with it, under
every parallel
of latitude, the
warmth and
light of the tropics.*

JOHN GREENLEAF WHITTIER

*... love is a wizard.
Submit to it faithfully
and it gives a person
joy. It intoxicates,
it envelops,
it isolates.*

LEOS JANÁČEK

*The countless generations
Like Autumn leaves go by:
Love only is eternal,
Love only does not die....*

HARRY KEMP

*... you have bereft me of
words,
Only my blood speaks to
you in my veins.*

WILLIAM SHAKESPEARE

*To love is to enjoy
seeing, touching,
and sensing with
all the senses....*

HENRY BEYLE STENDHAL

[A loving heart] plants its Eden in the wilderness and solitary place, and sows with flowers the gray desolation of rock and mosses.

JOHN GREENLEAF WHITTIER

We are empowered by sharing our deepest self with another person, offering him or her our heart, our soul, our life.

ELLEN SUE STERN

*Age does not
protect you from
love. But love to
some extent, protects
you from age.*

JEANNE MOREAU

To love someone

is to be the

only one to

see a miracle

invisible

to others.

FRANCOIS MAURIAC

Love, all alike,
no season knows,
nor clime
Nor hours, days,
months,
which are the rags
of time.

JOHN DONNE

... *we are made*
for loving:
all the sweets of
living are for
those that love.
Be joyful, unafraid!

THE RUBAIYAT OF
OMAR KHAYYAM

Treasure the love you receive above all. It will survive long after your gold and good health have vanished.

OG MANDINO

Love... that turns
Wilderness Row into
Paradise Place,
and Garlick Hill
to Mount Pleasant!

THOMAS HOOD

We love because
it's the only
true adventure.

NIKKI GIOVANNI

$\mathcal{D}$o what you will. Ignore it. Neglect it. Starve it. It's stronger than both of us together.

FROM "NOW, VOYAGER"

... this was what love was: this consecration, this curious uplifting, this sudden inexplicable joy, and this intolerable pain....

ANONYMOUS

In the arithmetic of love,

one plus one equals

everything and two minus

one equals nothing.

MIGNON McLAUGHLIN

No cord or cable can draw

so forcibly, or bind so fast,

as love can do with a

single thread.

ROBERT BURTON

[Love is]... a fire. But whether it is going to warm your hearth or burn down your house, you can't tell.

JOAN CRAWFORD

Love is always open arms.

With arms open you allow

love to come and go as it

wills, freely, for it'll do so

anyway.

LEO BUSCAGLIA

*Love bears all things,
believes all things,
hopes all things,
endures all things.
Love never ends.*

I CORINTHIANS 13:7

Were it not for love,
Poor life would be a ship not
worth the launching.

EDWIN ARLINGTON ROBINSON

*A*ny time that is

not spent on love

is wasted.

TASSO

*P*ains of love be
sweeter far
Than all other
pleasures are.

JOHN DRYDEN

*L*ove is a
universal migraine,
A bright stain on
the vision
Blotting out reason.

ROBERT GRAVES

Our love is like the misty rain that falls softly – but floods the river.

AFRICAN PROVERB

*In Love no
longer "Thou"
and "I" exist,
For self has passed
away in the
Beloved.*

FARID AL-DIN ATTAR

*I*f love wills to take on
another course, it goes:
and all the prisons,
guards, chains or
obstructions in the
world aren't strong
enough to detain it for
a second.

LEO BUSCAGLIA

*L*ove is spontaneous
and craves expression
through joy, through
beauty, through truth,
even through tears.

LEO BUSCAGLIA

*Couples who
love each other
tell each other
a thousand things
without talking.*

CHINESE PROVERB

*Love
is the
poetry
of the
senses.*

HONORE DE BALZAC

*L*ove alone is capable of
uniting living beings in
such a way as to complete
and fulfil them, for it alone
takes them and joins them
by what is deepest in
themselves.

PIERRE TEILHARD DE CHARDIN

Love is a short word,
but it contains all:
it means the body,
the soul, the life,
the entire being.

GUY DE MAUPASSANT

We are all born for love.
It is the principle of
existence.

BENJAMIN DISRAELI

Love is comfort in
sadness, quietness in ...
tumult, rest in weariness,
hope in despair.

MARION C. GARRETTY

*Because they have
been in love they
have survived
everything that life
could throw at
them....*

ERNEST HAVEMANN

*Take away love,
and our earth
is a tomb.*

ROBERT BROWNING

I don't want to live – I want to love first, and live incidentally.

ZELDA FITZGERALD

We feel [love] as we feel the warmth of the blood, we breathe it as we breathe the air, we carry it in ourselves as we carry our thoughts

GUY DE MAUPASSANT

Love feels no burden,
thinks nothing of trouble,
attempts what is above
its strength, pleads no
excuse of impossibility....

THOMAS A KEMPIS

*Two things cannot alter,
Since Time was,
nor today:
The flowing of water;
And Love's strange,
sweet way.*

JAPANESE LYRIC

*Love only
is eternal,
Love only
does not die....*

HARRY KEMP

Love seeks one thing only: the good of the one loved. It leaves all the other secondary effects to take care of themselves. Love, therefore, is its own reward.

THOMAS MERTON

*L*ove is the patient
architect that builds
*M*isunderstandings
into understanding.

OGDEN NASH

... I see her every day,

and always see her

for the first time.

JEAN RACINE

*There is only
one happiness
in life,
to love and
be loved.*

GEORGE SAND

Love
comforteth
like sunshine
after rain.

WILLIAM SHAKESPEARE

*Love is but the discovery
of ourselves in others,
and the delight in the
recognition.*

ALEXANDER SMITH

To love is the great Amulet that makes this world a garden.

ROBERT LOUIS STEVENSON

Love isn't decent. Love is glorious and shameless.

ELIZABETH VON ARNIM

To love abundantly
is to live forever.

HENRY DRUMMOND

Never forget that the most powerful force on earth is Love.

NELSON ROCKEFELLER

Time flies, suns rise, and shadows fall –
Let them go by, for love is over all.

FOUND ON A SUNDIAL

Love consists
in this: that two
solitudes protect
and touch and
greet each other.

RAINER MARIA RILKE

*Love... will put its hook
into your heart and force
you to know that of all
strong things nothing is
so strong, so irresistible,
as divine love.*

WILLIAM LAW

Love gives us in a

moment what we

can hardly attain

by effort after years

of toil.

JOHANN WOLFGANG VON GOETHE

'Tis love,
'tis love,
that makes
the world
go round!

LEWIS CARROLL

Who,
being loved,
is poor?

OSCAR WILDE

*Love is
when the
desire to
be desired
takes you
so badly
that you
feel you
could die
of it.*

HENRI DE TOULOUSE-LAUTREC

*Only love
can break
your heart.*

NEIL YOUNG

*B*y Love all are
bewildered,
stupefied....

FARID AL-DIN ATTAR

The madness of love is
the greatest of
heaven's blessings.

PLATO

*That is true love
which always and
forever remains the
same, whether one
grants it everything or
denies it everything.*

JOHANN WOLFGANG VON
GOETHE

You cannot touch love... but you feel the sweetness that it pours into everything.

ANNIE SULLIVAN

Many waters cannot quench love, neither can the floods drown it.

SONG OF SOLOMON 8:7

*Love, with little
hands, comes and
touches you
With a thousand
memories and asks
you
Beautiful,
unanswerable
questions*

CARL SANDBURG

... In our life there is a single color, as on an artist's palette, which provides the meaning of life and art. It is the color of love.

MARC CHAGALL

[Love] creates fragrance
in the air, ardor from
coldness, it beautifies
everything around it.

LEOS JANÁČEK

*I am loved: a message
clanging of a bell in
silence.*

JOYCE CAROL OATES

Oh! the heart that has truly loved never forgets.

THOMAS MOORE

The supreme happiness of life is the conviction of being loved for yourself, or, more correctly, being loved in spite of yourself.

VICTOR HUGO

The heart that loves is always young.

GREEK PROVERB

You have intensified all colours, heightened all beauty, deepened all delight. I love you more than life, my beauty, my wonder.

DUFF COOPER

Those who love deeply never grow old; they may die of old age, but they die young.

SIR ARTHUR WING PINERO

For finally, we are
as we love. It is love
that measures our
stature.

WILLIAM SLOANE COFFIN

The truth [is]
that there
is only one
terminal
dignity – love.

HELEN HAYES

Love may not make the world go round, but I must admit that it makes the ride worthwhile.

SEAN CONNERY